Baseball's GREATEST STARS

Clayton KERSHAW

by Matt Scheff

SportsZone
An Imprint of Abdo Publishing
abdopublishing.com

abdopublishing.com

Published by Abdo Publishing, a division of ABDO, PO Box 398166, Minneapolis, Minnesota 55439. Copyright © 2016 by Abdo Consulting Group, Inc. International copyrights reserved in all countries. No part of this book may be reproduced in any form without written permission from the publisher. SportsZone™ is a trademark and logo of Abdo Publishing.

Printed in the United States of America, North Mankato, Minnesota
082015
012016

Cover Photos: Pat Sullivan/AP Images, foreground; Morry Gash/AP Images, background
Interior Photos: Pat Sullivan/AP Images, 1 (foreground); Morry Gash/AP Images, 1 (background); Chris Williams/Icon Sportswire, 4-5, 6-7, 21, 26-27; Seth Poppel/Yearbook Library, 8, 9, 10-11, 12-13; Mike Janes/Four Seam Images/ AP Images, 14-15; Rich Pilling/MLB Photos/Getty Images, 16-17; Kevork Djansezian/AP Images, 18-19; Eric Risberg/AP Images, 20; Jae C. Hong/AP Images, 22, 23, 24, 25; Paul Sancya/AP Images, 28-29

Editor: Patrick Donnelly
Series Designer: Laura Polzin

Library of Congress Control Number: 2015945986

Cataloging-in-Publication Data
Scheff, Matt.
 Clayton Kershaw / Matt Scheff.
   p. cm. -- (Baseball's greatest stars)
Includes index.
ISBN 978-1-68078-076-5
1. Kershaw, Clayton--Juvenile literature. 2. Baseball players--United States--Biography--Juvenile literature.   I. Title.
796.357092--dc23
[B]   2015945986

CONTENTS

NO-HIT BID

Los Angeles Dodgers fans packed the stadium on June 18, 2014. Most were there to see baseball's best pitcher, Clayton Kershaw.

Kershaw dazzled the Colorado Rockies hitters. He retired the first 18 men he faced. Then Corey Dickerson hit a slow roller to start the seventh inning. Dodgers shortstop Hanley Ramirez scooped it up, but he fired wildly to first base. Dickerson reached second base on the error. Kershaw's bid for a perfect game was over.

FAST FACT

Kershaw became the first pitcher to strike out 15 or more hitters in a game without allowing a hit or walk.

Kershaw delivers a pitch to the last batter in his no-hitter against Colorado.

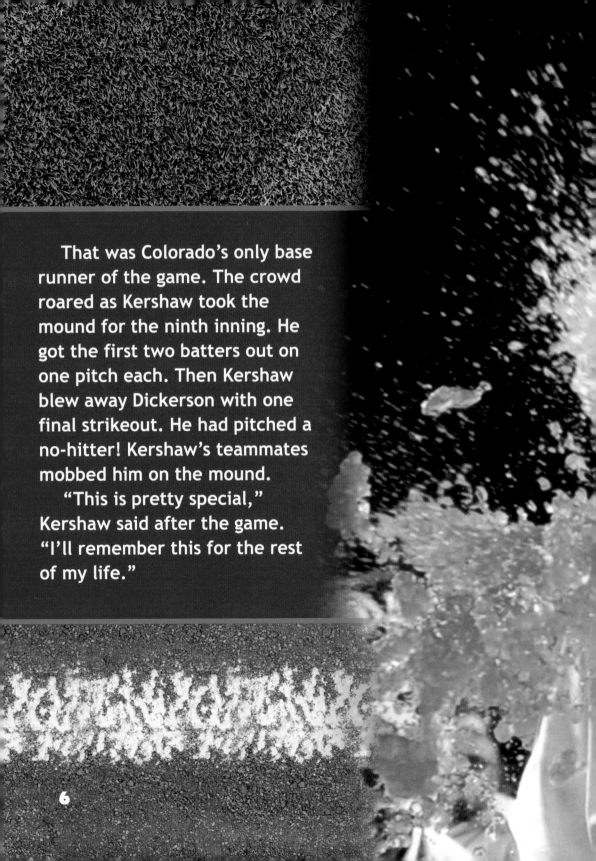

That was Colorado's only base runner of the game. The crowd roared as Kershaw took the mound for the ninth inning. He got the first two batters out on one pitch each. Then Kershaw blew away Dickerson with one final strikeout. He had pitched a no-hitter! Kershaw's teammates mobbed him on the mound.

"This is pretty special," Kershaw said after the game. "I'll remember this for the rest of my life."

Kershaw gets a Gatorade bath after he no-hit the Rockies.

EARLY LIFE

Clayton Edward Kershaw was born on March 19, 1988, in Dallas, Texas. His parents divorced when he was young. Clayton lived with his mom in nearby Highland Park. He was a natural athlete. He and his friends were always outside playing sports. They made up indoor games such as "hallway hockey" to play on rainy days.

Clayton grew up in Dallas, Texas, home of the Texas Rangers.

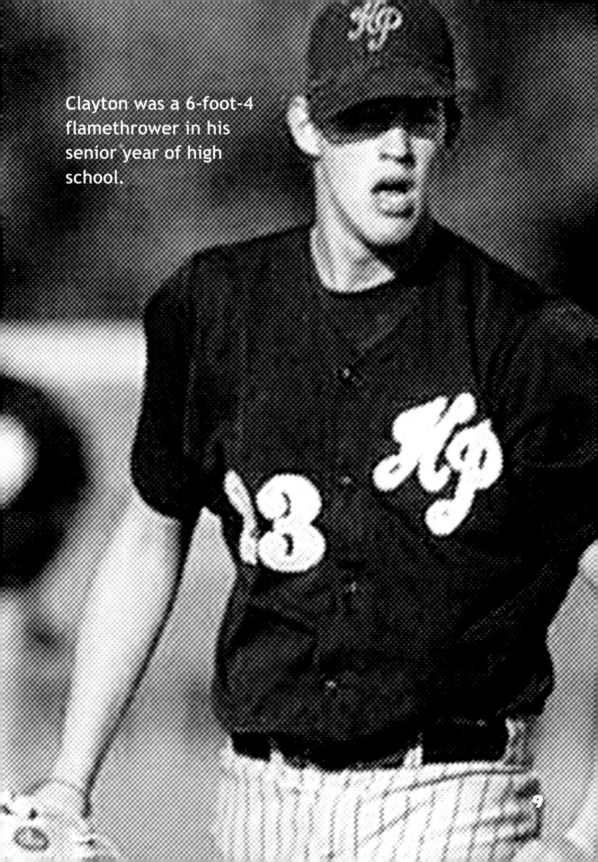

Clayton was a 6-foot-4 flamethrower in his senior year of high school.

Clayton played baseball for Highland Park High School. At first he relied on his great control on the mound. Then he went through a growth spurt after his junior year. His bigger body turned him into a true power pitcher. He went 13-0 as a senior. In one game, he struck out all 15 batters he faced. Clayton was a top prospect.

FAST FACT

One of Clayton's childhood friends was Matthew Stafford. Stafford now is a star National Football League quarterback.

Clayton loved to play
football when he was
growing up.

Clayton was gaining national attention. *USA Today* named him the 2006 National High School Player of the Year. Clayton planned to play baseball for Texas A&M. But he never made it to college. The Dodgers selected him with the seventh pick in the 2006 Major League Baseball Draft. He was headed to the pros!

FAST FACT

Clayton played center for Highland Park's football team.

Clayton, *top row, second from right,* was a star at Highland Park HS.

GOING PRO

The Dodgers sent Kershaw to the Gulf Coast League Dodgers. That is one of their minor league teams. He pitched just 37 innings for his new team in 2006. But he made a big impression. He froze opposing hitters with his curveball. Then he blew them away with a fastball that reached 96 miles per hour. Kershaw struck out 54 batters that season. And he walked only five.

FAST FACT
The Dodgers gave Kershaw approximately $2.3 million to sign with them.

Kershaw dazzled minor league hitters with his wicked curveball and blazing fastball.

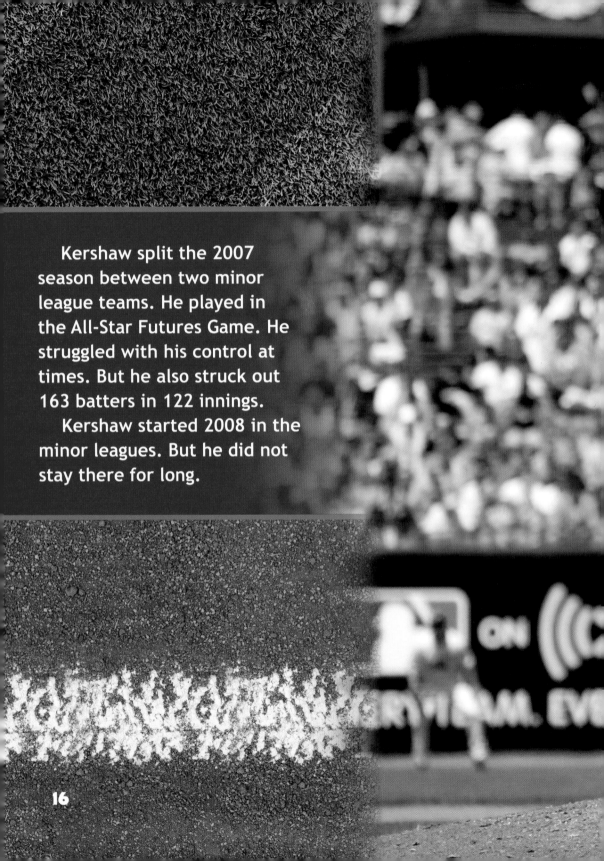

Kershaw split the 2007 season between two minor league teams. He played in the All-Star Futures Game. He struggled with his control at times. But he also struck out 163 batters in 122 innings.

Kershaw started 2008 in the minor leagues. But he did not stay there for long.

Kershaw represented Team USA in the 2007 MLB All-Star Futures Game in San Francisco.

THE BIG LEAGUES

The Dodgers called up the 20-year-old lefty on May 24, 2008. He made his first major league start the next afternoon. And he struck out the first batter he faced.

Kershaw went 5-5 in his rookie season. He even got a chance to come in as a relief pitcher in the playoffs.

Kershaw faced the St. Louis Cardinals in his major league debut on May 25, 2008.

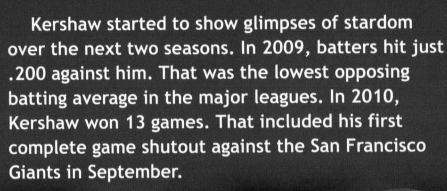

Kershaw started to show glimpses of stardom over the next two seasons. In 2009, batters hit just .200 against him. That was the lowest opposing batting average in the major leagues. In 2010, Kershaw won 13 games. That included his first complete game shutout against the San Francisco Giants in September.

Catcher Rod Barajas congratulates Kershaw after the lefty's first major league shutout.

FAST FACT
Kershaw married his longtime girlfriend, Ellen Melson, after the 2010 season.

Kershaw and his wife, Ellen, arrive at the 2012 ESPYs.

AWARD WINNER

Kershaw's real breakout season was 2011. The 23-year-old was dominant. He already had a great curveball and fastball. An improved slider left him with three deadly pitches. Opposing hitters were often helpless. Kershaw won the pitching triple crown in the National League (NL). That meant he led the league with 21 wins, a 2.21 earned-run average (ERA), and 248 strikeouts. He was named the NL Cy Young Award winner.

Kershaw won his first Cy Young Award in 2011.

CY YOUNG AWARD WINNER

2011

CLAYTON KERSH

Kershaw fires a pitch at Dodger Stadium.

FAST FACT

Kershaw wears jersey No. 22 in honor of his boyhood hero, slugger Will Clark.

Kershaw just kept rolling. He led the NL with an ERA of 2.53 in 2012. Then in 2013, he won his second Cy Young Award. Kershaw led the Dodgers back to the playoffs, too. They faced the Atlanta Braves. Kershaw struck out 12 batters in the first game and earned the win. The Dodgers advanced to the NL Championship Series. But Kershaw struggled. The Dodgers lost both games he started.

Kershaw rounds the bases after going deep on Opening Day in 2013.

Kershaw watches the ball fly after hitting his first major league home run.

FAST FACT

Kershaw is not known for his hitting. But in 2013, he belted his first major league home run.

Kershaw picked up the win in the Dodgers' 2014 season opener. Then a back injury forced him to miss more than a month. When he returned, he was almost unhittable. He went 21-3. His ERA was a jaw-dropping 1.77. He won his third Cy Young Award. And he became the first NL pitcher to be named Most Valuable Player (MVP) since 1968!

FAST FACT

Kershaw's great 2014 season ended with a thud. The Dodgers lost both playoff games he started.

Kershaw follows through on a pitch in a 2014 game.

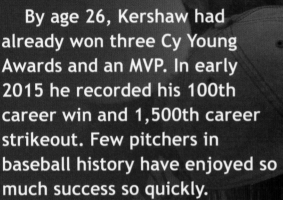

By age 26, Kershaw had already won three Cy Young Awards and an MVP. In early 2015 he recorded his 100th career win and 1,500th career strikeout. Few pitchers in baseball history have enjoyed so much success so quickly.

Kershaw's place as one of baseball's greats is already secure. How much more can he achieve? Dodger fans cannot wait to find out.

FAST FACT

Kershaw helped start an orphanage in the African country of Zambia. He named it Hope's Home after a child he met there.

Kershaw signs autographs for fans during spring training in Glendale, Arizona.

TIMELINE

1988
Clayton Edward Kershaw is born on March 19 in Dallas, Texas.

2006
Kershaw is named National High School Player of the Year. The Dodgers draft him seventh overall.

2008
Kershaw makes his major league debut. He posts a 5-5 record that season for the Dodgers.

2010
Kershaw tosses his first major league shutout against the San Francisco Giants.

2011
Kershaw wins the NL pitching triple crown and his first Cy Young Award.

2013
Kershaw wins his second Cy Young Award and leads the Dodgers to the playoffs. He also belts his first big-league home run.

2014
Kershaw has one of the greatest seasons for a pitcher in baseball history, winning his third Cy Young Award and the NL MVP.

2015
Kershaw wins his 100th career game and records his 1,500th career strikeout.

GLOSSARY

CONTROL
In baseball, a pitcher's ability to throw the ball on target.

CURVEBALL
A pitch that slightly changes direction during its flight toward the plate.

CY YOUNG AWARD
An award given every year to the best pitcher in the American League and National League.

DRAFT
The process by which leagues determine which teams will sign new players coming into the league.

EARNED-RUN AVERAGE (ERA)
The average number of earned runs that a pitcher gives up per nine innings.

PERFECT GAME
A game in which a pitcher retires every batter and allows no base runners.

PROSPECT
An athlete likely to succeed at the next level.

ROOKIE
A first-year player.

SCOUT
A person whose job is to evaluate talent.

SHUTOUT
A game in which a team scores no runs.

SLIDER
A pitch that often breaks down and away from the batter.

INDEX

ABOUT THE AUTHOR

Matt Scheff is an artist and author living in Alaska. He enjoys mountain climbing, deep-sea fishing, and curling up with his two Siberian huskies to watch baseball.